W9-BPP-487

Two SHORT, Two LONG

A Book About Rectangles

by Christianne C. Jones illustrated by Ronnie Rooney

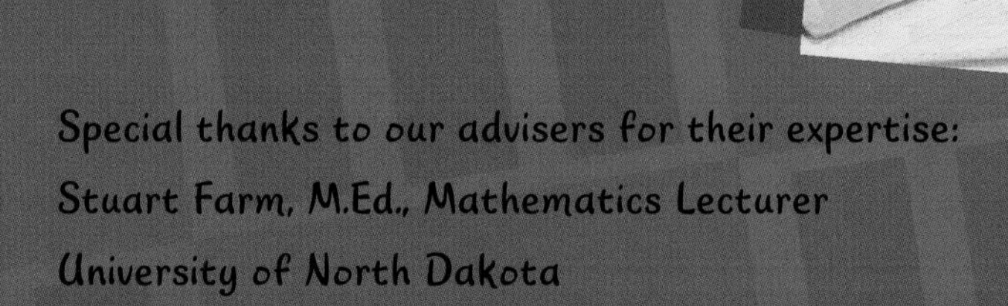
Special thanks to our advisers for their expertise:
Stuart Farm, M.Ed., Mathematics Lecturer
University of North Dakota

Susan Kesselring, M.A., Literacy Educator
Rosemount-Apple Valley-Eagan (Minnesota) School District

PICTURE WINDOW BOOKS
Minneapolis, Minnesota

Editor: Jill Kalz
Designer: Joe Anderson
Creative Director: Keith Griffin
Editorial Director: Carol Jones
The illustrations in this book were created in acrylic paints.

Picture Window Books
5115 Excelsior Boulevard
Suite 232
Minneapolis, MN 55416
877-845-8392
www.picturewindowbooks.com

Printed in the United States of America.

Library of Congress Cataloging-in-Publication Data
Jones, Christianne C.
Two short, two long : a book about rectangles / by Christianne C. Jones ; illustrated by Ronnie Rooney.
p. cm. – (Know your shapes)
Includes bibliographical references and index.
ISBN 1-4048-1573-2
1. Rectangles–Juvenile literature. I. Rooney, Ronnie, ill. II. Title.
QA482.J664 2006
516'.154–dc22

2005021846

Shapes are all around. You can find them everywhere you look. Shapes can be tall and skinny, short and round, long and wide. Some shapes will look the same, and some will look different, but they are all amazing.

Let's find some shapes!

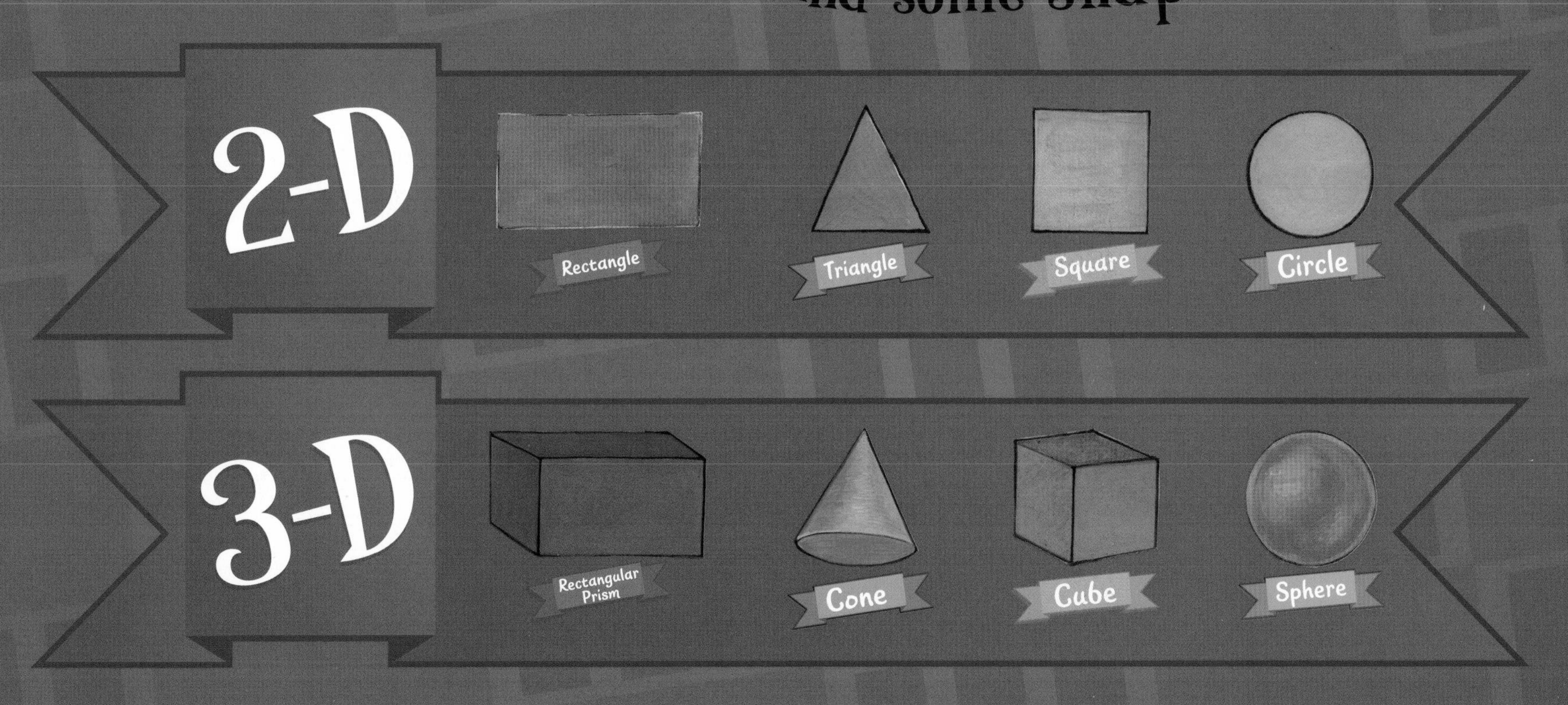

Two sides are **long**,
and two sides are **short**.
Rectangles are the subject
of my **report**.

A big yellow rectangle gives me a ride.

A **metal** rectangle
keeps supplies inside.

At a wooden rectangle is where I sit.

Clear **glass** **rectangles** help keep the room lit.

A **white** rectangle
teaches spelling and math.

JKLMNOPQ
WXYZ
+4=8
2
+5=
2+2
4+4
5+5

A smelly rectangle
holds all of our trash.

A **rope** rectangle keeps the teams apart.

Volleyball
Class

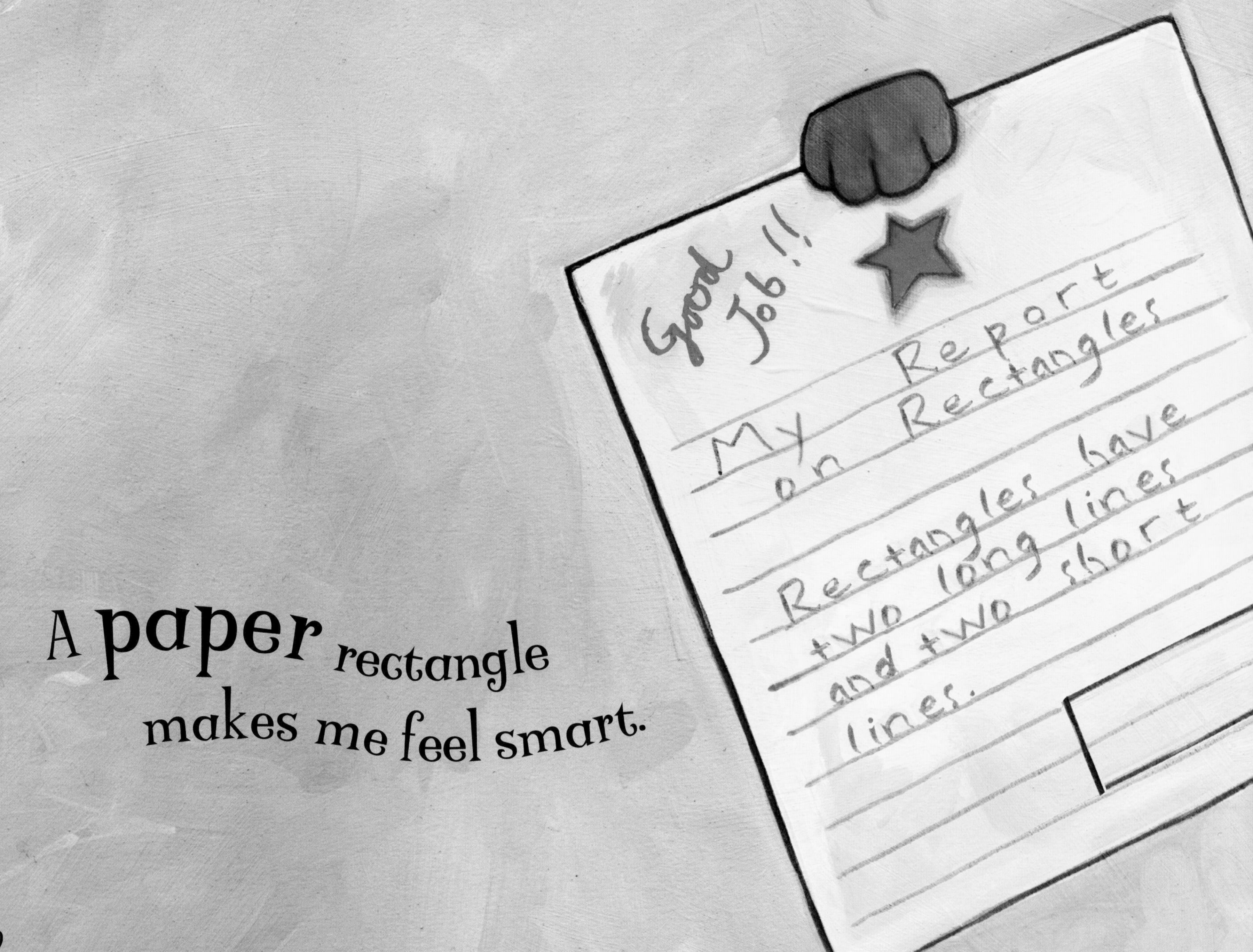

A **paper** rectangle makes me feel smart.

My day **at school** is already done.
But finding **rectangles**
has just **begun!**

STOP

RECTANGLE PUZZLE

WHAT YOU NEED:

- An empty cereal box
- A ruler
- A marker
- Scissors

WHAT YOU DO:

1. Have an adult cut off the front of the cereal box.
2. Use the ruler and marker to draw different shapes on it.
3. Have an adult cut along the lines to make puzzle pieces.
4. Now, put the pieces back together to make the rectangle. Have fun!

TO LEARN MORE

AT THE LIBRARY

Bruce, Lisa. *Patterns in the Park.* Chicago: Raintree, 2004.

Burke, Jennifer S. *Rectangles.* New York: Children's Press, 2000.

Schuette, Sarah L. *Rectangles.* Mankato, Minn.: A+ Books, 2003.

Scott, Janine. *The Shapes of Things.* Minneapolis: Compass Point Books, 2003.

ON THE WEB

FactHound offers a safe, fun way to find Internet sites related to this book. All of the sites on FactHound have been researched by our staff.

1. Visit *www.facthound.com*
2. Type in this special code for age-appropriate sites: 1404815732
3. Click on the FETCH IT button.

Your trusty FactHound will fetch the best sites for you!

FUN FACTS

- Two-dimensional (2-D) shapes are flat. They have just a front and a back. Three-dimensional (3-D) shapes have a front, a back, and sides. A rectangular prism is a 3-D rectangle.
- A ruler is a tool for measuring things. It is 1 foot, or 12 inches (30 centimeters), long.
- A Chinese man named Ts'ai Lun made the first pieces of paper nearly 2,000 years ago. Before then, people wrote on leaves and tree bark.

LOOK FOR ALL OF THE BOOKS IN THE KNOW YOUR SHAPES SERIES:

Around the Park: A Book About Circles 1-4048-1572-4

Four Sides the Same: A Book About Squares 1-4048-1574-0

Party of Three: A Book About Triangles 1-4048-1575-9

Two Short, Two Long: A Book About Rectangles 1-4048-1573-2